The Essence Of My Reflection

by Clifford Carolina

Edited by LLTE Editing

www.LLTE-EDIT.com

Richmond, VA

ISBN-13:
978-1494479824

ISBN-10:
1494479826

The Essence of my Reflection

Introduction •

First, I would like to thank God for allowing me to come so far in my life's journey. I'd also like to thank my family from the depth of my heart for believing in me, for their encouragement, and my sister Lucille's patience, along with their unconditional love. As I sit here thinking about the introduction to my book of poems- I thought how does one explain God's gifts. I say that because if someone would've told me 15 years ago that you would be the author of a book of poems- I would have told that person to get their head examined. But, God has his own plan.

The Essence of My Reflections is a group of expressions of my inner most thoughts and feelings about my experiences throughout life. "Parent Eternal" is about the flight of a soul while it is in the spirit form and before it enters the womb. After retiring from 30- years as a cardiac perfusionist, I was sitting in a beautiful resort that had four corners and I thought "where do I go from here" and at that time I wrote Four Corners of Paradise." Like many of us who lived through the 1950s through the Millennium- I have witnessed man's inhumanity towards man and the hurt and destruction that it has caused. So, I was encouraged to write "A Season of Hope." However, no amount of hatred could stop birds from singing, the flowers from growing and the rain from falling- so, I wrote "I Wonder Why the Birds Sing," "The Sound of Rain," and "The Lake Where the White Lilies Grow." My faith in God has a way of strengthening me and in honor of our God I wrote "The Presence of God" and "In the Hollow."

Lastly, all of my family is important to me more than I can say, but the loss of family members has taken that love to another level difficult to explain, so I wrote "If I Could See Forever," "How do I Let Go" and "Someone is Calling Me Away."

I pray that all who read my book will feel the spirit that I felt in writing it. To my wife Cleopatra, to my daughters Serena and Fatima, my sons Ronnie and Richard, son-in-law Erick and my beautiful grandchildren-

This book could not have been written without you. So with all of my heart and love I dedicate this book to you.

Author Clifford Carolina

A Season of Hope •

On these last few days of winter, a new season
approaches – A season of hope.
Not just for the people of the world who will be
awakened by the warmth of spring, but for the human beings
throughout this world who have endured this winter of despair and
man's inhumanity toward man.

I pray that God grants us his blessing, and give us grace. Just as spring
gave new life to fertile earth and intoxicates us with beauty that can
only be descried in a song or in poems...She comes to us with all of her
life giving lovely-ness—as a season of hope.

A season of new promise of peace, a chance for our children to dream
of things like love and kindness and simple human compassion for all of
the people of the world.
When we look at the earth and its relationship to the sun, the stars and
the universe – what we see is
perfect harmony.
Is there a question why there is no conflict?
Because in that beautiful phenomena lies the hand of God, in all of his
glory.
We as God's people look at this picture clearly, we will see our own
salvation.
Just like we will entertain our own destruction if we ignore it.

So with this new season of hope let us start again.
If we, who were created in his image can't come
together to bring about a   brighter future, then what hope is there for
the children?

When we think about tomorrow and the many beautiful days to follow –
let us build a foundation of good will for all people – no matter what
their race, religion, or ethnic background.

We human beings-leave a season of hope for our
children and our future.

Dedicated to my grandchildren

A River So Wide •

Just like the currents in the river, our life flow spirit is singing the harmony of every being. Take me. Please take me to the shore of my river, a river so wide. One that is bright with a new promise of a tomorrow of joy and happiness and peace that challenges our hearts and strengthens our soul, a river so wide.

So let us continue on this journey, asking and praying for wisdom and guidance so that we will become wiser and stronger, not forgetting that it is not just our bodies that need nurturing, but our mind and most importantly our spirit. Therefore, we flow not unlike the stream that empties into a river and makes up the whole body. So soulful is that natural and earthly act and so beautiful the simplicity, a river so wide.

So now that our goals are more clear and the distance not so great, let us continue on our journey, making stops along the way, but remembering every step of the way, it is not the shores end that is most important, but the journey itself.

Wonder Why the Birds Sing ●

If you could fly just like the birds above – some flying low and others
flying high. Some flying to tremendous heights beyond our eyes.
The view is so beautiful at that height – oh so different, yet the same.
If you could see through their eyes how would you express yourself?
Have you ever imagined in your deepest dreams how wonderful it
would be to see what they see?
I wonder why the birds sing?

They fly through the forests of the earth. They overhear conversation
among the animals of the woods. They dwell with the large and small.
They enjoy those privileges and sing. If you could join them on their
journey – what would you think – would you sing?

How great and wonderful this world is – room enough for us all, Space
for every living thing. The birds know it – do you?
They fly together – they fly apart – they stay in harmony with God's
earth. They question the confusion among us and still they sing.

I wonder why the birds sing?

If we could translate their beautiful sounds and songs, I am certain in
my heart that you would hear them giving praise to God and singing his
glory to the world.   If we could watch God's unfolding blessings like the
birds do –
there would never, ever be a doubt or wonder –
why the birds sing.

The Sound of Rain •

The sound of rain is a universal melody – one that speaks to us all, no matter what language you speak, not matter what color you are, not matter if you are a man or a woman. It sings your song, the sound of rain, the sound of rain, is falling.

Every drop of rain is sacred. It is our Fathers way of
saying "Let there be growth, drip, drop – let there be substance, drip, drop – let there be beauty, drip,
drop – let there be life. The rain is falling – there it is again – the sound of rain.

The rain is falling on barren lands – creating its own
rainbow. As if the entire earth itself was just a seed that needed just a little water to blossom.

Oh listen to it, not just with your ears – please feel it with your soul.

Recognize the gift, the rain is falling around you. The sound of rain. It is incredible the profound effect it has on our present state. Our future condition -
our lives today.

This rain, this rain – there it is again – the sound of rain. When the rain is over and the sun returns again –
will any of us remember this gift?

The beauty of the sound of rain.
It is raining in the garden – it is raining in our valleys. It is raining on the hills of life. To bring a more fruitful
tomorrow – God is in our presence.   The sound of rain.

The Lake Where the White Lilies Grow •

With the coming of spring, you see them around the lake and through
the enclave, off the shore, shortly after dawn. The fog is lifting and the
dew is on the grass. There is a touch of sunshine around the place
where the white lilies grow.
There is something strange, but beautiful about the
lilies- how they suddenly appear as if hiding in the
shadow of the forest around the bend and by the lake where the white
lilies grow.
They reveal themselves like a lover, a quiet whisper of
seduction in your ear of new things to come. Hiding their real beauty
and floating in a scent of mystery. Oh, how I wonder about the flowers
around the lake where the
lilies grow.
On a cool spring day we are down by the lake drifting, quickly
meditating about the events of the passing day. The birds are singing
and the butterflies are beginning to show themselves. The earth itself is
screaming to us- awake its spring and you are beautiful and alive. Give
vent to the beauty inside of you and then you will realize the part you
play in this lovely mosaic that makes up the harmony of life.
Oh, those beautiful flowers around the lake where the white lilies grow,
and when this wonderful spring is over and summer really begins, you
will find with a closer inspection that the lilies are not white at all- but a
colorful, beautiful flower that cleverly fooled us all. Yet, I still
wonder about those extraordinary flowers around the lake where the
lilies grow.

Dedicated to my niece Lisa

Parent Eternal •

I was drifting in space, somewhere in the universe, going nowhere, when my   creator called me and gave me a home. Finally I am home, after wandering through so many dimensions, not knowing where my destination would be. I am safe. I am home.

Thank you. I have found my parent.

Isn't is strange that we human beings cannot distinguish the spirit from the soul or the body from the spirit. Until we find ourselves in the safety of the womb, parent eternal.

Drowning in some indescribable beauty – drifting through the stars, a memory of a tasteless journey was I whole. Was I complete? Something is guiding me – but to what end.

There is a feeling of certainty. There are vibes. There is a knowing that I am a part of something very special. The rapture of beauty is over-whelming. Am I falling, Am I out of control or my place of arrival pre-destined. Are the sounds I am   hearing and feeling real or are they some song of the universe screaming in my soul, come home my son – I am waiting. Parent eternal

I am so comfortable, so at peace. I am happy. I am
crying. I am screaming. Oh My God - am going or I coming? Is this a beginning or is this the end.
Parent eternal.

So Many Parts •

There are so many parts of us – it is hard to explain where we begin and where we end. On part dying to live and other living to die.

Do we know where one part ends and the other begins. Our thoughts and desires flowing in every direction. Our spirit in another. The melody in our soul is the same – yet we are out of step with it – dancing, yes dancing to a strange and different tune.

Why cannot these parts come together. There are so many parts. It is hard to   explain where one begins and the other ends.   Sometimes it is irrelevant with what we do with one part if we ignore the other because off of our parts compliment one another.

There are so many parts it is hard to explain where one part begins and the other ends. Last night my spirit was soaring, seeing another adventure, another mystery,
another place, I know not where.   So many parts – you cannot even imagine where they begin and where they end.

Suddenly, something happened sand for some reason they all come together and we feel and we know it is real because for a moment we are complete.

These parts, these parts, so many of them. It is
impossible to tell where one part begins and the other ends.

Tomorrow •

Peering at the pale blue light, awakening from a long, long night,
Tossing and turning – coming out of a restless dream of one's
subconscious mind. The mixture of smell and aroma intoxicates me.
The sweetness of dawn, unable to determine light from
darkness, consciousness from unconsciousness. Am I still dreaming or
am I awake? A longing for tomorrow, tomorrow. I dream about
tomorrow.

A brand new day beginning – what mysteries will it hold, what new chal-
lenge will it bring? A sudden surge of energy. A moment of quiet
excitement, awakening me even more. Still as I lay here thinking of my
dream of the night that is passing...I wonder what were these
confusing pictures in my restless dream that fill my every moment just
before dawn. Did I confess my deepest secrets and if so, to whom?

Then without warning, the mind becomes as clear as still cool water, and
all of your troubles drift away, just before tomorrow.

What strangers fill my sleep and who were they, I wonder. Were they
old acquaintances from yesterday – gone by or quiet clues of future new
encounters.

Tomorrow, tomorrow, I dream about tomorrow. A new day, a chance to
dream again.

As Night Falls •

What is so strange about this beautiful night – that it grows brighter the
late later it gets.
Why is this night so special. Why does it hold me in its arms caressing
my every thought. It embraces the mystery of the night but grants the
cleaners of daylight. How strange this wonderful and lovely night.

All the activities of the day is slowly losing its energy to the darkness
that is crying out for the night. The moon like a director suddenly
appears to give light to all that embraces the darkness as night falls.

I am a part of this phenomena, just as the stars, moon and the
beckoning aura that created this sweet and intoxicating beauty that is
this night. As night falls I am clothed in its mystery and swallowed in its
secrets. I walk around the people of the night joining them. Laughing
and dancing, rejoicing and celebrating this beautiful night. As night
falls, let's embrace this beautiful moment and hold each other tight, so
part of this lovely night will live between us forever.

Let us explore the wonder of this exquisite and blissful night. I am so
enthralled and so caught up with all that is happening around me. I
seek less of the daylight and more of the night.

As night falls...

The Quiet Toro ●

On this beautiful day far out in the woods, he stands.
Alone, moody, undecided. He moves with a quiet
regality.
But, with a fearful demeanor.
What my God is troubling this huge beast?
The forest is alive with all kinds of activity.
The birds are singing – the butterflies are out with their beautiful wings
in masses.
The smaller animals are going about their day.
It is almost like the woods are trying to calm this beast.
But alas, in vain it is also obvious to note how unstable this animal
seems to be that life in the forest continues as usual.
It is not strange how lives for many of God's creatures are in harmony
with the universe?
I wonder who is out of step with God's plans?
He Strides back and forth as if he is wresting with what direction he
should go within himself. Suddenly he stops.
What hinders him, is he wresting with direction or could it be good and
bad.
Is Toro's confusion real or is it symbolic of man's
struggle with good and evil.
If positive deeds are determined by the direction you choose –
Than we plead O Lord – go in the direction of good.
All of the children today and tomorrow are praying...

Make your choice good El Toro.

Dedicated to Pastor, Willie R. Jones •

He's chosen our earth out of all of the stars in the
universe -
to give us his personal and supreme grace.
He then ordered a larger star to be our sun -
to provide all that is needed to sustain life. To determine our night from
day, he has done all of these things to show his children his love.
Oh look what he has done.

When we his children stop for a moment to look around us, when we
can hear and see and with all of our natural senses we can feel his
presence.
Then, in a quiet moment of the night, like a time selected by him, we
realize that we have been blessed.
Oh look what he has done.

He has taken us, a people that have everything of value, taken from us,
our soul and spirit, that have been broken and separated ton apart, but
through his grace we are still here. Oh Jesus, I'll savior, "Look what he
has done".

He has bought us through the valleys of persecution and death, when
just about every soul on earth turned away.
He continued to carry his children –
"Oh look what he has done".

Now that the morning light is draining and darkness begins to fall,
he lights up the night with brightness to allow us to see his power and
to full our life with his grace.
He has allowed us to gather in his beautiful sanctuary to sing and to
praise his name.

He has provided a Shepard among us to honor his
precious name.
Oh look what he has done.

And after many years of labor cradle in the arms of the Lord, he has
traveled through the storms of changes held on to his faith and

continued to preach the word of our savior, "Kings of kings, Lords of
Lords", our key to the kingdom of heaven, the baby Jesus Christ.
Oh look what he has done.

And during his trials and tribulations,
when physically ill and when many thought his heart would fail,
God showed his faithful servant his love, and said "rise up my son,
you're healed.
And now we celebrate this anniversary in recognition of his dedication
and work, to show our love and
appreciation – The angel of this church...
Oh, look what he has done

A Friend ●

A friend, what is a friend, and how would one describe that person?
A real friend is first – a gift from God.
One whom you can depend on in times of needs, when the tides of life
is low.
A friend can lift you up with their concern and compassion
Brightening your outlook and change your day with their
Understanding and their sincerity.
A confidant that you can reveal your most secret concerns and desires.
Your dreams of yesterday and tomorrow. Oh yes,
That is a friend.

When you have joy in your life – when god blesses you with good
fortune, a friend celebrates your luck and your accomplishments.
They will cheer your presence and miss you when you are not there.
Sometimes when our hearts are full and our minds are confused, that
person who is your comrade and true friend can stir and help direct you
to a more peaceful and quiet place where there is balance and love.

In acknowledging all of those wonderful qualities that make up a friend-
be careful to realize like all of us –
whoever that person may be – he or she –
are imperfect and has flaws,
only our " Heavenly Father" is that entity in our life that is perfect and
always remember
"God is the ultimate friend."

In the Hollow •

When we look around us and seek what is beautiful, we sometimes
wonder where is this evasive love our spirit longs for and so we dream.
If we would just look within us and drink in the natural beauty that is
there we would know deep in the hollow of heart there is love. Take
this. Please take this walk with me through life. A journey that has led
us here. Across rivers and lakes. Through valleys and over hills and
mountains we have come. Why have we come this way? Why this
place?

There is nothing really here, but we know somewhere in the Hollow –
there is peace.
This morning all of the birds are singing with different sounds and
different noises but yet in harmony. They are saluting you and celebrat-
ing life and you can hear it.

Rejoice, rejoice, there is no sadness here.

For we all know deep in the hollow – there is joy. Still wondering
through life – seeking that special path, one that will complete us and
make our spirit Happy because we know somewhere in the hollow –
there is truth.

God is walking among us – who is he? Do not ask where he is, just look
at each other and you will find Deep in the hollow of your soul – there is
God.

To Whom Do You Turn •

When you are confused and nothing seems right, when all that you hold dear seems to turn away, when you awake in the morning instead of light youperceive darkness.

Then something ha affected your very soul, when so much you cherish and love is out of sight or out of reach and all you can hold on to are pictures in your mind of yesterday's gone by.

What then do you do for the strength and hope to carry on. You fall to your knees, hold on to your faith and turn to your God.

He has been patiently waiting for you, His child, to comfort, to love, to guide and to forgive. To take you in His arms and give you peace.

He and he alone knows you best, when he created us with all of our human emotions – He knew that you should love someone with every feeling in your very being, that your heart is on fire when that person is present.

He knows that you must laugh because that is the way to express joy and happiness. He knows that you must cry to rid yourself of the sadness that possesses you.

But with supreme understanding and compassion, He will mend your heart and heal His child – so never lose faith in yourself and your Father who has created us all. Turn to Him and you will find Him here.

The Presence of God •

The beauty of a sunset – a rainbow in the mist

The appearance of a butterfly – the sound of a Robin.

The birth of a Child – the miracle of Life.

THE PRESENCE OF GOD

Is it not strange how soft and sweet the images are, yet with Gods hands on

Them – so powerful the effect.

A song that touches one's heart – the sudden appearance of a love one

THE PRESENCE OF GOD is all around us.

The seasons change – The transition from Spring to Summer – from Fall

To winter.

The splendor of a new day – another chance to enjoy GOD'S PRESENCE.

A family gathering the essence of love and unity and hope.

THE PRESENCE OF GOD, I tell you. Bath yourself in it's Beauty & Power.

Know at that moment what it is trying to make you realize

THE PRESENCE OF GOD in you.

Can you feel it – Can you hear it – Can you touch it ?

The angels are singing and the Heavens are crying out !

IT IS THE PRESENCE OF GOD IN YOU .

The Essence of My Reflection •

I see some strange and wonderful world, filled with love and hope.
Simple human compassion – a world without wars.
A world where the natural fruits of the earth are shared with all of its
people. I see this through the eyes of my reflections.

I see this beautiful place with my heart and my spirit. All of us-black,
white brown, red, and yellow dancing together in joy. It maybe with a
different rhythm, but all in harmony. Just imagine that!

A party where God is the conductor and the entire world is his stage. I
see this serene and wonderful utopia through the essence of my
reflections. From the depth of my soul and my very being, I feel it.
Love, peace and understanding. It is my rock in which every relationship
succeeds under. And it is God's command. If one would just realize
that we are here to further life and move on there would be no fear of
death, just a better appreciation of life.

So then let us sing the songs of love. Cradle in our arms this moment
and just allow it to live. Pray that the flame that started it never dies.
Please do not tamper with it. For there is imaginable beauty and it
supplies us with our every need.

All of this I feel and see through --
the essence of my reflection.

I feel this great stillness, within this vastness.
The quietness of the moment. Just the slightest movement of the wind
awakening me from my thoughts. This – this is the time, this is surely
the time with our father's guidance we shall all be free--
Free from Hatred
Free from Racism
Free from Hunger
Free from War
Free from Self -destruction

I see God's hand on this, and all of this I see through --
the essence of my reflection.

Four Corners of Paradise •

Sitting here looking at four corners by the sea-
I began to examine my life and its real meaning.
Its goals, its accomplishments and failures...

And so I decided to ask at this crossroad in my life...
Who are you? Where are you going from here? And where best could I
question myself? I though – where better than this place by the sea?

How many people am I a part of? Who have I touched?
Who am I responsible for? Who am I?

So, in this beautiful place surrounded by four corners of the sea, I face
my future and my destiny.

Sitting here I look upward at the sky. I see two clouds passing one
another. One is dark and the other is bright. Each has a meaning. Is
that the way one's life evolves? I wonder, since neither cloud has
control over its path nor where it was going. Do we have any control
over our destiny? But somewhere beyond the cloud lies the
answer.

In these four corners by the sea...I dwelled into my soul and found
paradise.

Someone Is Calling Me Away •

As we live from day to day. As we enjoy our life and seek to hold on to the ones we love, as we endeavor to reach out to others as we pray, some one is calling us away. In what direction should I go when so many things are tempting, should I give in to my weaker desires and let the winds of change sweep me up. When suddenly a small voice within me screams "Stop you are traveling in the wrong direction". Then I dwell deep down in my soul, and pray father which way, something further much deeper than that answers my child you are blessed. Oh yes, yes my lord, as soon as aid get down on my knees – I know father I am healed.

Something loving beautiful and supreme is calling me away. How does one feel when they are whole completely in tuned with their mind and spirit, it's impossible to explain if you have never been healed, touched by our father giving grace by our savior, wrapped in the arms of the Lord. And just like that, just in a magical moment – it is clear. Why am I here and who I really am. What is my purpose for living? Oh yes, yes, sown deep in my soul – a voice is quietly calling me away.

Sometimes when I am alone and all of the noises of the day are silent and I am completely still, I often wonder who designed this sacred tomb that my mind and soul dwell in, the answer comes its like a mighty wave – a clap of thunder. Who but our father my child, and then all of the hurt and pain – the agony of life slips away and then I am alone and totally at peace with the one who is calling me away.

If I Could See Forever •

If I could see forever how wonderful it would be
I thought as I looked into the ocean of eternal motion
How far this water has traveled, how much land it has touched, how
many lives has it nourished
If I had the strength of the ocean and the wisdom of the sea
If I could see forever – how wonderful it would be
In my spiritual minds eye – I see many doors, each leading to some
heavenly journey
Which one will I choose

As I sit here thinking deeply – I sipped a glass of wine
Blinded by indecision, I wondered over and over again
As my thoughts rolled over like cumulous clouds
Is there clarity. Is there time. If I could see forever, how wonderful it
would be

Some bridges lead from one bad situation to another
Some lead to new adventures, new possibilities – a whole new life
And, there are doors that open to love, understanding and compassion
Which one will I choose

If the scope of my vision was as large as the sea and as deep as
the ocean
If I could see forever, how wonderful it would be
As I sit reflecting on the journey of the hills and mountains that has
brought me to my present.

I realize that my journey has been my window into that shore, so close
but ever so distant.
If I could see forever how wonderful it would be -
my Lord.

How Will I Let Go ●

How does one let go when your heart is breaking and the person that

you miss so much is gone – from this earth and forever in your heart?

Then I felt your spiritual presence and in doing so

realized there is a way....

When I look in the face of your children I see you.

When I look at your grandchildren I see you.

When I look at your work I see your gift.

I see your smile, your laughter, your vision.

All paint a portrait of you.

So what is it that I am really saying - that everything about you is here

Except what we miss the most – your presence.

It is so selfish of us – being such an infinite speck in this enormous

phenomena – called the Universe.

To think that GOD would choose to touch us and bring us peace.

Then I realize that we all are his children and that harmony is his rule.

A wise man once told me "that in the winter the earth swallows the

seeds of Life enriching them and feeding them in her bosom

until the spring pushes them back above the ground giving us new

hope, new beauty and new life.

We are one family under GOD holding on close to what unites us and

avoiding what divides us.

We shall survive – thinking through this cloud of pain and loss.

Remember the promise of the Resurrection – knowing God's Law.

This healing begins knowing that the soul of our love one is a part of

this great universe – and it lives, we can then begin to let go.

Dedicated to the Family

Made in the USA
San Bernardino, CA
15 February 2014